# Shadow-feast

*Also by Joan Houlihan*

*Ay*
*The Us*
*The Mending Worm*
*Hand-Held Executions: Poems & Essays*

# Shadow-feast

## JOAN HOULIHAN

Four Way Books
Tribeca

Names: Houlihan, Joan, 1951- author.

Title: Shadow-feast / Joan Houlihan.

Description: New York, NY : Four Way Books, [2018]

Identifiers: LCCN 2017029365 | ISBN 9781945588082 (pbk. : alk. paper)

Classification: LCC PS3608.O85545 A6 2018 | DDC 811/.6--dc23

LC record available at https://lccn.loc.gov/2017029365

This book is manufactured in the United States of America and printed on acid-free paper.

Four Way Books is a not-for-profit literary press. We are grateful for the assistance
we receive from individual donors, public arts agencies, and private foundations.

PROUD MEMBER

# [clmp]

We are a proud member of the Community of Literary Magazines and Presses.

Distributed by University Press of New England
One Court Street, Lebanon, NH 03766

"Once daily at a fixed hour, she would set for the absent husband, in his favorite room, little repasts faultlessly served on dainty lacquered trays, miniature meals such as are offered to the ghosts of the ancestors, and to the gods. Such a repast, offered to the spirit of the absent one loved, is called a Kage-zen or Shadow-feast."

Lafcadio Hearn, *Kokoro: Hints and Echoes of Japanese Inner Life*, pub.1896. (Tuttle Publishing, 2005).

In Memory of Eric Mayorga Howlett

Contents

Hers

His

Theirs

Hers

SLEPT OUT to sea and sailing in a wave
uncertain what was in the hold      then comes from years: a comb,
a roof, a bowl of him and she,   she slept on a deck gone under.
It was no ship. It had not hold.                The only way to keep him, hand
or eyelid, was to rise. She met               each step with his. She ate
her part and his, stirred and kept him      to a cup of tea, finger handle worn
by him, the rim, the rim  he also put his mouth to, the steam

                              a moist full breath to the nose.

HANDS TRACE AIR-knots, ropes.
*Scaffold. There's no fixing it.*
His bed-thought hurtles
its rails, his boyhood train
smokes, coils away.
*Tuck the blanket under my chin.*
What does he feel going cold?
Room-gust, my hand passing over?
Awake on a shore where it's never the future,
afraid he will last no longer,
he goes down a stair in his chest.
*Give me a mirror so I can see behind me.*

ON THE OTHER SIDE of our body     things jingle, drop
through the wall. Curtains rush,           a slow splash, then
sticky squares dab.        Time came in and stranded us here.
We creaked open, listening.     The past stacked high on us,
day looked into us.      Clarity without remedy. To rescind,
to wind back clean as wind,     I would give anything.
         Beneath our lids, other eyes.

SEWN INTO SHADOW, he looked out older.
Urge ghosted him. She sat him up to sip
a bowl of broth—
maple at the window, each leaf lit—
when to lie down was all he wanted.

THEN MORTAR was mortification
because of the marbled veins in it,
the crack from turning and grinding,
fist on pestle, my force not enough,
some pieces uncrushed
not even dissolving in water.
The hurry to get them into your mouth
and then you would not swallow.
Like a sprung chest, a body opens,
empties itself at the last.
Let it be lost. Let it pass.
Where you are, you went alone
as cloud huddled cloud, muscled then blown.
This cramp in my hand is from grinding,
from crushing small pills smaller,
from stirring clouds into water.

HE IS WALKING the wind again,
eye drawn down, unsure
as the dark comes over. Hard to see
in his mysterium, his singledom,
the misguided lot of him, quieted.
His cloud-worship and feel for the dog,
their garble of bark and ridge, his seeing
a leaf-stem to its swift twist, all
make him kinder to himself now, familiar
to his own hands around a bowl.

AS HOME GRIPS the body      he is pitch looked into
and the room a dread to enter.     Tongs hold parts
of what the limbs belong to      as if there would be more.
        Effaced, they are each the other.

AWOKE OUT from inside
Coughed sideways
*Look into me*
*Touch my side*
*My throat, choked*
*It is I    It is I*
*Going*

BY EYE-SLIT, by blood-drum, by clumsy pats along your arm,
by bracing thighs and heaving up, you almost stood, but slumped.
I listen to you sleep, sawn limbs whispering wood to the head,
assemblage of the parts you came from. Someone else in this room,
unfed, no end to his wound, flies from you.
His home is not this home.

COME TO THE WAIT and the sea
brims and laps, a full-throated froth
is near, as we float
without guile or a yet-to-come.
a body, slow behind
and the sound of it far and faint.
trails in our own boat's wake.
Your shut eyes, your cannot see.

flexes sleek in the sun,
and we know the other
benign on a breeze
Born of what sun we followed,
attached to us but the rope is long
At night, a silhouette stuck on the moon
My shut eyes, my cannot see.
The white of its head, bobbing.

AS IN A SACK held shut by cord,
what wasted you, hid in you,
fell quiet each day, ready for us.
Your pain wasn't physical, hadn't taken you.
Your body wasn't yours but a made one.
Nothing pierced far enough to matter.
Drip, and a softening torture
brought us together.  Stretched-out arms
felt with fingers for a way out.

## WHAT DOES YOUR SEEING WANT?

Your scrunched eye seizes, sizes
me up: pulley-roped palliatives, craft and lies.
Washing my hands in the back, I wonder:
what's a good death?
Of course you held on and I held on to you.
We had married ourselves to a trance.

STICK FIGURE, knee-boned, you
step off the scale—
*Almost to my high school weight!*
Your smile so fake it breaks me.
We count, withhold, endure.
Skin without mind, tissue-
timed, blood and detritus—
slow murder.  What ate you away
keeps on eating.

THE ROOM
The chair
The body
The suffering
To the top of his head

THE WORK OF YOU, wound-sealed,
strapped, needled deep by a feeder, a taker—
what medicine surges, strips you,
stills the red spill to its pouch?
You wheedle, *when?* and remain naive—
*let's make a plan*—believe
in food and paper, keep one finger on the call-button,
nod to the walker—*my ticket out*—
but all you have is this tray and cup.
*Move it closer. Day passes. Now move it away.*

TOO SMALL for his own robe now, bowed
and listening to pump and pulse,
he lets the spoon fall to his lap.
*Help me stand!* Awake,

I am bound to his call but wait, wait it out,
until he won't quiet and I rise again to struggle
him forward, inch by inch to the edge, then
hook and hoist him from under the armpits

until he is almost up, then: *no, no I can't. Let me down.*
And I can't be there every hour and the hours
I am not he sheds years like peonies, rag-
tipped in their last attachment to stem until one,
beetled with holes you can look through,
will not fall—*Help me stand up!*—
and how cruel that he sleeps in a crib-sided bed,
rattles the sides, and what stirs in him when he sleeps,

what sentry hears the century
slip, knows how far, how small,
how shrunken a clot of *no* he is. But there's no going back,
he is past the time of incision, past being drained and left

to dry, and still he will not comply, shrunken to a diorama
of a man stooped, intent, fingers fitting screws into girders,
working unfazed and content
as if the frame will soon fill with concrete blocks
lifted and set in solid testimony to a world—

and when will I see him
softer, not hard-handled, but feeling
the light that grew him, that warmed his desire to stay.

STILL HEARD in her head: *They burn what's left.*
And then he is there again: hands to face,
shut off and steeped in *no.* His terrible angle of shoulders,
her insistence, sham of control, as what couldn't be cured or fed
turns wasting from a bowl. She served him as mother, as wife,
forced to bear up his frame, collapsed. *Stand up. You can do it.*
His trying to do what she asked.

BREATH HE WORE
On ribs bolted small.
*I choke on.        Drown in.*
*Rise away,*
*Bone.*

A STILL-LIVING HEAD of hair.
Body no longer his. No order
shines within it. The mantel candle huddles
as she turns him, lantern of bone, dabs
with soapy cloth, each part of him, which is a god.
Tube and tape pull off, widen the stain on the sheet.
Thrust leg and leg into pants, his own.
Thrust arm and arm into sleeve. Button his shirt,
collar to cuff, then clip off a piece of hair.
He does not move. At dawn the birds come up,
and the smell of rain-eaten dirt.

DON'T ASK HOW LONG he felt.
Ask how long he could see.

The bag billowed red to its bottom,
poured out and pouring
its river of going

and her hands moved across him
sternum to rib

as he stretched out silent, carved in extremis,
translucent, skin-lit, pearled.

She moved through the room on church feet
shadowed by no better choice.

His whole body opening,
the hours delivering, pouring their minutes
onto each other, pouring and pooling

toward evening, after
the rash push of day.

Of heat that is not in the world
Of an age that passed over and left her—

Don't ask how the room looked after.
The chair with its loose nest of tubes.

When they came for him full-dressed
and somber, they lifted a body made lighter

by suffering, laid it into the rubber bag
then zipped it to the top of his head.

DECEMBER KISSED the year goodbye and tossed us into winter.
I was behind, without you. You went ahead into the lie we kept.
And who knew the whole of it, minded us, cared?
I am hollow as it made me. I am walked and circled and startled.
Is this the way we leave it? Who will give me grit and will
and who will help me live it? It wasn't sleep, it isn't sleep.
I haven't risen, I rise. No one told us, but I tell all.
Do you remember the last cure? It nailed your thinking shut.
Do you remember the ground, our root? All our feet were cut.
I remember how we huddled, shivering, clothes full of snow.
How you then, kingly, all in white, let go.

IN THE SNOW OF having found him
listening to the cold that is him
as he froze in a gesture of *no* and said
*the man I no longer am—*
She waited to hear the rest.
There was no rest and nothing but ice on the window.
Caught in a storm born of his last breath,
she heard the bottom of the world crack.

His

AWOKE DARK, lung-snared, creaked out a cry.
No one heard me. Took my winded climb up from inside.
Coughed and blistered there, aired by a window,
and they came sideways to look into my last eye:
*He is the same.* They left the eaten cities inside,
left famine to work its way through.
Buildings drop, glands touch and talk.
Out of my side, sewage. Out of my throat, the choked streets.
Please don't leave. It is I, a deluge, drained to a bucket,
and out of my eye, the labored light of a going sun.

*IS ANYONE hurting you?*
Leave me. I am work. I am legs.
I am horse shackled to cart.

      *Do you know what year it is?*
Yes. It is lung. It is pump.
It is high hiss and squeal.

      *How do you feel?*
Each part of me feels for floor.
I am floor and cough.
I am father in a long coat dragging.

      *Do you know who you are?*
Fist-gripped onto wheels I am
Made of what makes my voice.
*You* are hurting me.

WOULD BE MY ARMS, my trunk.
My age and all I came from.
No page as thumbed as I am.
And what was farther north,
the latitudes I loved—up in smoke.
Lean me on you, I am rid of wish.
The earth is worthless.
The earth is beneath me.
Heard my head say *hollow.* No.
Heard my head say *hole,* and then
the cold air through.
They say I cannot speak.
They say it's winter and I have another name.
Call it moaning, call it melting.
I'm gone as soon as you get here.

YOU WERE RIGHT. I couldn't climb
the stairs. Breath was all I wore,
ribs rose in and out, and what bolted my body together,
poor meat, was a small will. Smaller than me.
But I'll prove I live. I am mute, but thought-loud:
look at me, this freight I am.
No air I don't choke on. No bed I don't drown in.
I need to rise but my legs are away.
Then my bone split, spoke: *what night is this?*

A LATE WASH and I looked a parch, a curse,
an ancient continent stained on wallpaper.
A part of me began to leak. Whose body rains
like that, tethered to a grunt, inched and shifted, tugged
and rolled? The man we saw was me.
The mouth we made, the name I tried to form
of you, the hand we held, our own,
the bandaged book we read from, ours too.

VOICES, LATELY. They scare me.
Rummage my sleep.
Steal my box of coins and teeth.
Hold it to their ears and shake
to hear the money.
A year ago, buds thrust and day
feathered our walls.
Now I'm the only ghost you know.
In night I sway before I fall.

COVER THE SOFT
*Walking from my body*
*Limbs, awake. Elbows*
*Arms, collarbones*
*The quiet.*

UNMOORED, AND EVER
only halfway there,
I rang for a boat
and sailed backwards on it.
Nothing for me here.
Only water, only mouth.
I am nod, I am torn, I am socket.
I am hellbent on heaven.
On whatever you believe.
What do you believe?
What I believe is a valley.
What's low lives there.

WHEN THE COUGH had burnt enough,
they used the soot to coat my throat.
It isn't sleep I get but rest. Remember him?
The gentle man who tore the air
and would not quiet?
When I sleep I'll lay my head
where his head once lay.

SMELL THE WIDE SMELL of split sticks burning.
I've always liked to watch a fire.
The light I beg for tightens then opens.
Are you spooked? Come watch me rise
through my head. Come catch me.
I won't come back down.

I WON'T QUIT. I'm your breath. The ache
in your legs and chest. What hums in you unsnuffed
while I blow away. Uncontained, as warm as wind
and spread to the eye, the gladiolas I saw as a boy.
Looking from a window in my first house,
I hold you here, where I am.

Theirs

BREATH THEY COULDN'T catch, motion that fell
as a run of shadow on their window
folded into one wish. Time—what was that—
flung over mountains where sun could blink and waver it off.
Clouds muscled in to not let them see the bald sky lying.
The knife-cold privacy exposed a man, and from his window
no motion, just New England birch, stripped limbs in late light.

AND ALIVE BETWEEN them, what was it?
Not the man, turned toward

his torn side. Not the woman, curious
to what wound had found him.

But a presence, pent and spectral,
strung with old words, rare to hold,

a flimsy skin made of her and him. Never alone,
she felt it. After the man is gone, it goes too.

SNOW-LIGHT CHILL begins a kind of home,
a lifted drift, a hill they could lie down on.
Still herself, nicked hands and fingers pale
from fret and his too: eyes tissue-blue,
slow-teared, and his snow-whipped hair—
her beautiful polar bear. Their snowbank crawled
with shadow, their crawlspace tight and squeaky
packed against what would come.
They had each other and the one they drag, his breath
on their tongues, blown blue, head a box-wire
strung with voice. Wrists poked out,
ankles raw, pants and shirt too big.
He lurched and swayed. The look on his face baffled
and lost. Botched man. They stuffed frost
in their mouths so not to laugh, kept him alive in their huddle,
brought fire for him, brought want for him, warming
his ice-block chest with their palms, murmuring hotly
into his neck: *don't go.* A low gurgle worked his throat,
and his body, about to be grit, about to be sifted,
about to be ash sharp with busted bones, finally went.
No home but what he left, spent.

JAMMED HASP loosened, the body
wants to come back. She coaxed him out
of his last-worn shirt, the ruined sheet.
They went so far north their teeth hurt, so far
the burnt hole meant sun.
At their backs a blown warble split out
of bark, the last of their lilac age.

*KISSED*
*Hollow*
*Near the end      I rise*
  *Remember*
  *Remember*
*How shivering white*
*I go*

NO FIRE to autumn's oak              apple-stray or leaf.

Dipped instead in pitch: their life, the one they forged

and stood beside.          No longer the manner

in which they lived,      calling each other home—

they are talked out, fallen through       a machine that nicks them sleepless,

knowing *cold* to mean a coming frost      and junked into a constant eddy,

the rasp of him          before his voice is gone.

*A DROWSE*
   *In the dark—*
*Cut root*
*Lives here.*

BEFORE THE INNER breath ceases,
lay him down on his side.
When the throbbing stops, he will come through.
Through cave and trough, through tunnel and well,
through funnel and valley, through the crown frontanelle,
in the time it takes to eat a meal.

His relief from breathing, from moving,
from hearing ringing and buzzing,
from seeing light attending,
in a calm abiding, without horizon.
Not unhurt, past hurt. Himself a carving,
a mask, a husk, a shoe to fill with flesh of foot,
a sink to fill with water and wash,
a grave, a hole, a box of ash.

1.

ONLY A FUNNEL of lung. Only
a hole where the eye hides
and below the cheek
the roots of his teeth—
whether his spirit can speak or not
I sense the flame by finger-lengths:
What distance from the navel.
What from the legs, the chest.
What from the tissue formed of muscle, thick
so fire can hardly harm it.
From the narrow canal of colon, the heights
and breadths of intestines, his.
The venous testicles, nested penis.
The size of a wide vein closing.
The muscles that tightened his mouth, across.
The million movements of his tongue.
The membranes that clothed his brain.
Dura mater. Pia mater. Vertabrae and spine.
When he no longer speaks, I listen.
In the might of my wish
and the thought of his thoughts,
I hear the noise of rain,

how it shatters the air.
(Withstand it.)
How it goes when it goes.
(Withstand it.)
And all this is known in the case of fire:
How in the first smoke is a power,
in the last a dying away.

2

In that first winter without you,
mist knit its vapors together,
touched the cut roots closer.
Without the help of your lips, tongue
or teeth, without your brain and heart,
I am back down the years
into faces we had, then
to what faced us down—
from the foot to the crown of you, soldered
then split, poured into a box
the heft of a brick
and handed to me as a gift.

ABOUT THE ENDURE I have, the panic
I have, no plot I have to receive it, no stone I have
to mark it, no circulatory no ambulatory, no shaking
I have, no light-filling day, what cannot be touched
I have, and where will he walk? How will he walk?
I have given his shoes away.

LAID ON A RACK of metal,
rolled into the chamber face up
then two to three hours in a rain of flame.
Don't be quiet like that.
Don't be stoic like that.
This listening cramps my neck.

COVER THE SIDEWALK with sawdust, so I am soft
in my walking. Phantoms grow from my body,
transparent limbs, perturbed awake. Elbows bend
in memory of arms, collarbones cradle the neck.
Tell the head and the body will follow.
Cover the window, quiet the talk.

WHO IS YOUR NAME, what is your home—
two years gone and your jacket still hung
at the end of my endless day.
And I know better than to call for you,
know better than to reach for you,
not in a grave, not intact,
but bedded in a burning, blacked.

IN THE SHIRT YOU WORE, that you never wore,
the hours, ponderous, stopped. Now you are sensate in me—
you, only whole, who altered earth away from me.
Once-blunt footsteps put your walk here again,
but quiet, quiet. And loose in this room
undoctored, a cranial arc and glow,
your forehead, face, leonine and kind.

WITH A DAMP DRAWN to him and a whistle
not in this world, whitening the jawbone shelved in his face,
whitening the knucklebone sheathed in his hand,
he rises with effort out of what's twisted,
straightens to upright and walks as he couldn't.
Through stitched breath he asks, *where am I?*
Still living on nerve, in my nerve.
I am too twisted to straighten.

IF HE CAME BACK talking, laughing off
the soot and small hallways where he had to crouch
and squirm to get through, not fearing close space
as when he lived, to come on the keepsakes: miniature dog
in full point, initialed spoon, an old globe, three copper screws,
mashed landscape from a train set—
how did they all fit in? Now he has his brown study, all the quiet
he wants, and no one can distract him from his thought-
work, whirr and pulse of machine in machine, nobody
to bother him with origin or end, as if he has his first mind, not his last.

WITHOUT HAND-HOLD or leg-hold,
hearth-tender and in full kilter,
he would be the gathering in her head,
the grave inside she tends and tends,
the one that is blackening soft.

TO SEE THE LOOK he gave going she closed her eyes.

Will you speak to me after, she asked, like rivers with trees underneath?

The look, the moan in his throat, one word too many caught round his mind.

We are nothing but mind after all, she thought.

AFTER IT COMES to calm
a sound remains in the bell.

Acknowledgments

My thanks to the editors of the following journals in which some of these
poems first appeared:
*Academy of American Poets Poem-a-day, At Length, Literary Matters:
Association of Literary Scholars, Critics, and Writers, Massachusetts Review,
Ocean State Review, Plume,* and *SPOKE.*


"By Eye-slit," "No Fire," and "Would Come Back," appeared in *The World
is Charged: Poetic Engagements with Gerard Manley Hopkins,* Clemson
University Press.

Joan Houlihan's four previous books of poetry include *Hand-Held Executions* (Del Sol Press, 2003), re-released in 2009 in an expanded version to include all her critical essays from Boston Comment; *The Mending Worm* (2006), winner of the Green Rose Award from New Issues Press; *The Us* (Tupelo Press, 2009), a poetic sequence spoken in the collective voice of nomadic hunter-gatherers at the threshold of language, named a 2009 must-read by the Massachusetts Center for the Book; and the sequel *Ay* (Tupelo Press, 2014). In addition to publishing in a wide array of journals, including *Boston Review, Columbia: A Journal of Literature and Arts, Gettysburg Review, Gulf Coast, Harvard Review, Poetry*, and *SPOKE: Irish and Irish-American Poets in Boston*, her poems have been anthologized in *Iowa Anthology of New American Poetries*, Reginald Shepherd, ed. (University of Iowa Press, 2005); *The Book of Irish-American Poetry, 18th Century to Present*, Daniel Tobin, ed. (University of Notre Dame, 2007); and *The World Is Charged: Poetic Engagements with Gerard Manley Hopkins*, William Wright and Daniel Westover, eds. (Clemson University Press, 2016).

Publication of this book was made possible by grants and donations. We are also grateful to those individuals who participated in our 2017 Build a Book Program. They are:

Anonymous (6), Evan Archer, Sally Ball, Jan Bender-Zanoni, Zeke Berman, Kristina Bicher, Laurel Blossom, Carol Blum, Betsy Bonner, Mary Brancaccio, Lee Briccetti, Deirdre Brill, Anthony Cappo, Carla & Steven Carlson, Caroline Carlson, Stephanie Chang, Tina Chang, Liza Charlesworth, Maxwell Dana, Machi Davis, Marjorie Deninger, Lukas Fauset, Monica Ferrell, Emily Flitter, Jennifer Franklin, Martha Webster & Robert Fuentes, Chuck Gillett, Dorothy Goldman, Dr. Lauri Grossman, Naomi Guttman & Jonathan Mead, Steven Haas, Mary Heilner, Hermann Hesse, Deming Holleran, Nathaniel Hutner, Janet Jackson, Christopher Kempf, David Lee, Jen Levitt, Howard Levy, Owen Lewis, Paul Lisicky, Sara London & Dean Albarelli, David Long, Katie Longofono, Cynthia Lowen, Ralph & Mary Ann Lowen, Donna Masini, Louise Mathias, Catherine McArthur, Nathan McClain, Gregory McDonald, Britt Melewski, Kamilah Moon, Carolyn Murdoch, Rebecca & Daniel Okrent, Tracey Orick, Zachary Pace, Gregory Pardlo, Allyson Paty, Marcia & Chris Pelletiere, Taylor Pitts, Eileen Pollack, Barbara Preminger, Kevin Prufer, Vinode Ramgopal, Martha Rhodes, Roni & Richard Schotter, Peter & Jill Schireson, Soraya Shalforoosh, Peggy Shinner, James Snyder & Krista Fragos, Megan Staffel, Alice St. Claire-Long, Robin Taylor, Marjorie & Lew Tesser, Boris Thomas, Judith Thurman, Susan Walton, Calvin Wei, Abby Wender, Bill Wenthe, Allison Benis White, Elizabeth Whittlesey, Hao Wu, Monica Youn, and Leah Zander.